RENOVATE

A 40 DAY DEVOTIONAL JOURNAL
TO RENEW THE MIND

SHANTE TRIBBETT

GODZCHILD PUBLICATIONS

Published by Godzchild Publications
a division of Godzchild, Inc.
22 Halleck St., Newark, NJ 07104
www.godzchildproductions.net

Printed in the United States of America 2020 - 1st Edition

Library of Congress Cataloging-in-Publications Data
Renovate: A 40 Day Devotional Journal to Renew the Mind

ISBN-13 978-1-937391-43-0

1. Shante 2. Tribbett

2020

TABLE OF Contents

FOREWORD
Tye Tribbett (Husband)

When my wife walked up to me to tell me that the Lord had called her to 40 days of consecration, I immediately agreed with that word as she started her first day. This is no real surprise to me though. We're talking about a woman born from the rural streets of Camden, New Jersey to parents who were not together. At an early age, she learned to seek the Lord for answers to life. By the time I met her, she'd developed into what I thought was one of the most beautiful, humble, honest, and most real young ladies I'd ever met! She's the same now... only BETTER! She is a daughter, a sister, a niece, a cousin, a friend, AND EVEN a wife, a mother, a mentor, a pastor, an advisor, a business owner AND now an author.

With over 20 years in marriage, over 18 years as a mother/guardian, over 30 years following the

Lord, and over 15 years in successful businesses, I assure you that, as you read this book, you will find the guidance, reminders, and lessons you need to liVe life the way God intended you to live... MORE abundantly.

I've watched this young woman. For over 20 years, I've had a front row seat. To know her is to know her humility, her kindness, her generosity, her authenticity and the list goes on. She's fun, she's loving, she's just an all-around DECENT person. She loves to take road trips (at least once a year) and try new things. She loves interior decorating and landscaping etc. (hence, the theme of the book*smile*). She loves her family immensely and she's a giver. You can always find Shante giving something: from advice, to kind words, to resources, to wisdom, to the clothes in her closet. Whatever she has, she gives! Which now brings us to this most recent gift from her... *Renovate!*

I can tell in her eyes that something significant was going to happen through this 40 day encounter with God. It just felt different when she told me (plus we had had a disagreement earlier so I definitely wanted her to pray *laughs*), and I also aligned myself to prepare to hear the word of the Lord. She would come to the room

DAILY, after her time with God, to tell me what was experienced. I honestly remember, on several occasions, wishing she had written it down or out it in a book! Here we are, a year later and you are reading this!!!!

I believe in this book because, number one, I know the author's heart for God's people. If she didn't think it would help anyone, she would NOT have published it. Number two: I know the author's testimony! I literally watched her go through this process and live out the perspectives you're about to read in this book. And I've personally seen it work firsthand! The spirit of fear has been destroyed over her life! And God has restored and renewed her life through this renovation process. She's a whole new Shante and I love it!

Which brings me to the third reason I believe in this devotional journey. In this covid-19 pandemic, while quarantined, God spoke to me while I was praying and He told me to "take the journey." I instantly knew exactly what He was talking about. He was telling me to read RENOVATE for the next 40 days. I had not yet read the finished product, because I wanted to kind of "save it" for the big "release day" or something, I don't know. All I know is He told me to read it now! Here it is, a Wednesday night and I'm currently on day 4 as I write this. The renovation has begun in me and I'm already loving the results! God has tag-teamed with my wife on this book to restore my soul! And let me tell you, I cannot be more grateful. Let them tag-team on restoring yours, too, as you flip through the rest of the pages to be refreshed, revived, renewed and Renovate(d).

My love, congratulations on your first release. This will be the first of many! The time has come, babe! I'm loving this new you, this GOD-you! Be blessed as you serve the people of God. ALL your needs are met. I love you! LETS GOOOOOOOOOO time to #RENOVATE

ACKNOWLEDGMENTS

To my heavenly Father, I give you glory for Life and strength. Thank you for truly being living water to my soul. I wouldn't be alive today had you not healed me and set me free from the bondage of guilt and shame that I carried my whole life. Your Son, Jesus was the ultimate sacrifice for my sins, and I'm free because of it. I now have access to all that you have stored away for me because you helped me build my faith in you. Thank you for the grace to consistently be able to renew my mind through your word. I'm a witness to your patience and amazing love. I Love, because you first loved me.

To husband, (my earthly friend) after 23 years of marriage, words can't express the width, height and depth of love I've experienced through you. I know without a doubt that God loves me because he gave me to you, to cover and take care of me while I was on this earth, and you've done just that. I couldn't have asked for a better human being to take this journey called life with. I'll love you forever.

To my lovely daughter, Austyn Tayler, our first born. You are very special to us. It was a delight to raise you. Your wisdom will carry you through life. Stay focused on pleasing the Father and He will give you the desires of your heart.

To my adorable daughter, Lyncoln Victoria, our second born. You are one of the most intelligent young ladies I know. Your father and I love you. God has healed you from many illnesses, so continue to prosper and be in good health as your soul propers.

Camary (God-daughter), Dad and I have loved you since you were in your mother's belly. We chose you before we even met you. God knows all things. You have been the perfect addition to the family and We're HAPPY to have you.

Special note: Mom, I'm here because of you. I wouldn't replace you with any other mother on this earth. I've only ever seen you work nonstop to provide for my brother and I. I've learned how to be a strong, well-rounded woman of God, because of you. I pray you will see the fruits of your labor.

LiVe Church! thank you for all of the love and support you never cease to show me. I'm honored to serve you. The Lord is with us; therefore, we will not fail.

INTRODUCTION

Hello, my readers! I pray this book finds you well. All of the information in this book was documented during my 40-day wilderness journey with God.

At the time, I had no intentions of sharing my experience, but I knew for some reason this journey needed to be written down. I took God's offer seriously because I was desperate for understanding. I needed to know what was actually happening. During those 40 days, God spoke to me from the inside, (the secret place). Without fail, each morning God would wake me up to talk to me. He would shine light on the hidden places in my heart. I saw things I would have never seen before had I not taken this 40-day journey with Him.

I've never been able to stick to much of anything for 40 days straight, but I heard God when He asked me to do it. *I had to use big faith.* I believed if I was consistent in the journey, it would make all the difference in the way I see and think, and it did. The Father is always ready to lead us to truth, we just have to do our part in preparing for it. Faith without works is dead faith. My prayer is that throughout this journey, you will begin to see transformation in your life too.

Let's continue...

So I developed a heart disease called hypertension, by way of anxiety, which meant my blood pressure was consistently and abnormally high. For many years, I struggle with symptoms like: headaches, blurred visions, tiredness, dizziness, nausea and sometimes, chest pain and vomiting. Between hypertension and the anxiety, those were all the things that plagued my day to day, making it hard for me to rest and enjoy life. When I was told I had hypertension, I was around 30 years old. I was in disbelief. I didn't understand why it was happening to me. As time went on, the hypertension got worse. It got so bad to the point where nothing or no one could help me balance it. I tried doctors in New Jersey and I tried doctors in Florida! The Doctors did their best, but it wasn't enough to totally heal me. At that point, fear began to creep in because I didn't know what was going to happen next. I was in a very humbling position. With no real relief from my symptoms, I came to the end of my search. The doctors did all that they could do. The medicine wouldn't work like I had hoped it would.

As time went on, I began to hear God speak. I heard Him say, "It was ME who made you, and no one else." When I heard that from within, it stopped me in my tracks. I knew it was God. This wasn't a position for man. This was a job only God could handle.

God had a strategy for me. He told me if I would just consecrate myself to him for 40 days, HE would make me whole. It was such a real moment, I had to respond to it. This is where the 40-day journey began.

First, things first: I shared the great news with my husband about what I had heard from God. When I told him, he was immediately supportive. Then, I sat my daughters down, and shared with them what was going on. They knew I had been sick for a while, but they didn't realize my condition was at its worst point. Once I spoke to my family about the 40-day journey, I began to gather my things and prepare for those 40 days with God.

The preparation for the journey went like this: I packed a small bag with all of my tools in it, things like a journal, a notebook and whatever reinforcements like the Bible and any other self-help books I had. However, I knew that my faith and focus was going to be most important.

My home office is where I planted myself for the 40 days. Yes, it was an extreme gesture, but I had to stay focused about the task ahead. Note: everyone's journey is different. You may not need to steal away for 40 days, but you can still take the 40-day journey with your regularly scheduled lifestyle. In my mind, I needed to do something extreme to get extreme results.

Once I settled into the office, I remember me saying to God, "*If this is you, please give me the strength to endure for these 40 days.*" Note: I didn't do a complete fast from food, but I did fast from sugar, unhealthy carbohydrates, fried and fatty protein. I only drank water and tea with local honey. From the first day, I heard God speak to me every single day without fail. I heard more from God in these 40 days than I did in my 40 years of living!

What God told me and what he did for me was unforgettable and unexplainable, but I'll do my best to share as much as I remember in this book.

As I take you through the 40-day journey, you will begin to see things differently, and more clearly. Ever since, I walked through this journey with the Father, I have become more of a faith-filled believer, with a fresh new outlook on life. This journey has definitely built my faith and has given me boldness and zeal to spread the gospel of truth for as long as I live.

God is good.

I pray that you get to know your heavenly Father in a better way through my 40-day journey devotional book.

Let's begin this journey...are you ready?

Day 1

THAT NEW NEW

Create in me a clean heart, O God; and renew a right spirit within me.

PSALM 51:10

I have yet to meet anyone who doesn't like new things. We'll that's me! I personally get excited and go into a 2-step dance when I get something new. I never really enjoyed old things like old houses and old cars, not out of vanity, but because I was always afraid that old things would break down and soon stop functioning altogether. Very often, things break down on us because we haven't kept up with the maintenance service of maintaining it. We blame the deterioration on the age and assume we need everything to be new; brand new, or what we used to call in the early 2000's, "that new new." But sometimes what is really needed is a full demolition and renovation. I hope today that you will stop and let God do a full demo and reno in you.

Here is a major point I want you to remember: God often wants to use the Word as a boulder or a wrecking ball to some of the mess we have allowed to cake up and tarnish our hearts. God wants to renew us inside, by first tearing up some of that old stuff so it can be restored.

As women in particular, we spend much time taking care of everyone and everything else, but we are weak at taking care of ourselves. As for men, some don't take the time to care for themselves because it could go against some of their cultural norms to do so. David knew of God's renewing power so he prayed "Renew in me a right spirit!" God knows who we are and He made us the way we are on purpose. God doesn't want to throw you away and start all over with somebody new. God has invested too much into you. You are the apple of His eye. He wants you to become everything He planned from the beginning. You got that "new new" on the inside, so let God bring it out of you.

Prayer: *Create in me a clean heart, O God, and renew a right spirit within me. Cast me not away from your presence and take not your Holy Spirit from me. Restore to me the joy of your salvation and uphold me with a willing spirit. In Jesus name, Amen.*

RENOVATION QUESTIONS:

1. Are you willing to give God free reign over your life and to let God change any and everything He wants to change?

   _____

   _____

   _____

   _____

2. Meditate on Psalm 8 and Psalm 51 today to be reminded that you are too important to God for Him to give up on you.

   _____

   _____

   _____

   _____

Day 2

RETRAIN YOUR BRAIN

Be not conformed to this world but be ye transformed by the renewing of your mind, that by testing you may discern what is the will of God, what is good and acceptable and perfect.
ROMANS 12:2

Have you ever tried to accomplish a goal, but you kept falling short? Have you ever tried to get rid of a bad habit, but you weren't able to win against it? Maybe you wanted to be a better steward of your body or conquer temptation in a particular area, but it just wouldn't take. Often times, the reason we are unsuccessful in our attempts at transformation is because we pursue new things with an old mindset. You are the total sum of what and how you think. What you think on constantly, you will become. Therefore, in order to become something new, we have to renew our minds, or retrain our brains to think new thoughts.

In order to retrain your brain, it is important to understand that your brain is not your mind. They do work together, however. The brain is physical and the mind is spiritual. The brain houses brain waves initiated by experiences and thoughts. Consistent exposure to whatever it is your working on becoming will inspire particular kinds of thoughts through specific experiences. The mind, on the other hand is changed by renewing it with the truth of God's word. Philippians 4:8 gives us an excellent strategy for renewing our minds. It tells us to think on things that are true, honest, just, pure, and lovely which are all acceptable to God. By doing this we teach ourselves to think differently, which leads to renewing of our minds. These words, experiences and thoughts train the brain to think in a new way, ultimately transforming our behaviors.

Now that you understand how to transform your mind, it is important to remember that the reason for the transformation is to become more like Christ. That takes consistency and focus. When we're born into this world, we're born in a sinful nature turned away from God the Father. He knows that our natural ways are at enmity with his ways. If we don't renovate our minds, then we won't be able to discern the good, acceptable, and perfect will of God. With the combination of renewing your mind and retraining your brain, I can assure you that you'll be able to accomplish all you desire. That's what renovation is all about. Like a house that needs an upgrade, we are hauling out the old unproductive and ungodly thoughts in our minds and replacing them with the new.

> **Prayer:** *Father I thank you for this day, which is the first day of my renovation journey. I thank you that you make all things new and give us the ability to be new by meditating on your holy word. Help me to be more like Jesus through the renewing of my mind. I thank you that through your strength and through your word, I will be victorious in all you said I could accomplished. In Jesus name, Amen.*

RENOVATION QUESTIONS:

1. What are some of the negative thought patterns that you are holding on to? What are some scriptures that you can meditate on in order to let go of those thoughts?

_____

_____

_____

2. What are some new goals that you would like to accomplish within the next year? What are two strategies from this lesson that you can use to reach these goals?

_____

_____

_____

_____

IDENTITY

Yet for us there is one God, the Father, from whom are all things and for whom we exist, and one Lord, Jesus Christ, through whom are all things and through whom we exist.

1 CORINTHIANS 8:6

Your identity is your most prized possession. It is the thing that separates you from others. No one else is the exact same as you. Even if you are an identical twin, you still have your own fingerprint. Nobody else has the same makeup, gifts, or the same personality as you. When God made you, He broke the mold. We are all custom-made by God and we exist for God. He is our Father and we are his children through Christ. OK! Let's get back to identity.

Identity can only come from one person or entity. Having an identity is like having an army behind you to help you fight through loneliness or anything that could possibly overtake you. We have to learn to lean into who God is and made us to be. God-given identity is the supreme identity in which we can rest. Once we understand that the only wise God is in us and we are in Him, then we will greatly benefit from it. Without God's identity we will develop unprotected. Growing up I didn't know that I even had an identity. My biological father was not in my home, and not having your father in your home is one of the biggest tricks of the enemy.

The enemy preys on people who don't have an identity, because identity only comes from your father, or the one who protected and raised you. Because I didn't have my biological father around as much, I grew up fearful and full of shame. I developed several dysfunctions that stayed with me all the way until my adult years. But while I was going through the dysfunction of my father not being there, God began to teach me how to navigate through life without a biological father. The circumstances surrounding Jesus' birth are relatable to those born out of wedlock and those whose biological fathers aren't in the picture. This is why Jesus draws even closer to the ones who have been abandoned. He too understands. The Bible says He draws near to a contrite heart and a broken spirit. As our example, Jesus never complained about not having an earthly father. Instead He spent that time acknowledging His heavenly Father. May we be careful to do the same thing today.

Prayer: *Lord, don't let me ever forget that my identity is found in You alone. No matter how we came into this world and what people think of us, we are God's precious children. Remind us every day of how much You love us all, right where we are. In Jesus name, Amen.*

RENOVATION QUESTIONS:

1. How did your experience with or without your father affect your life and the way you think?

_____

_____

_____

_____

_____

_____

2. What is something unique about your identity, that you believe makes you special?

_____

_____

_____

_____

_____

_____

Day 4

TAKE IT PERSONAL

For whatever was written in the former days was written for our instruction, that through endurance and through the encouragement of the scriptures we might have hope.

ROMANS 15:4

During my 40-day walk with God, He revealed to me that my faith was weak and that I needed to make it stronger. In that season, I had not yet totally believed the fullness of the Scriptures. He told me that I needed to start taking the word of God personally and He was right. I was a person who didn't believe that I deserved God's goodness, and that His promises didn't apply to me because I believed the enemy's words over God's word at that time. I was giving more energy to the words of people who were spreading lies and spewing negativity about me, and that was hindering my spiritual growth.

Not believing the word of God is dangerous to the development of our faith. Even though the bible was written by people long ago, it still applies to us. We must commit ourselves to read the Word daily with spiritual lenses to comprehend and effectively apply it to our lives, especially if we want to come against what the enemy has to say.

In 1 Corinthians 10:11, it says the Bible was written for instruction for the person who believes in it. The condemnation you hear from the enemy of your soul are words that are NOT to be taken personally, but the word of God should ALWAYS be taken personally. His words are true and only the truth will make us free. Spending more time studying the Word has helped me realize this: only God's word matters.

> **Prayer:** *Lord Jesus, I thank You for all of Your promises in Your word. I pray today that You would help me to see and hear You and to give me the power to cast down any negative thought or word that comes from the lies of the enemy. I believe Your word is the only word I should take personally so I can move forward in my faith. In Jesus name, Amen.*

RENOVATION QUESTIONS:

1. Is it easier for you to receive something negative about yourself rather than something positive? If so, why do you think that is?

   _____

   _____

   _____

   _____

   _____

2. What person or story in the Bible do you connect with most? How can that story or person help you in your life today?

   _____

   _____

   _____

   _____

Day 5

BEHIND THE WHEEL

Now oh Lord you are our Father, we are the clay, and thou are the potter; and we are all the work of thy Hand.

Isaiah 64:8

Do you remember when you first learned how to drive? Remember how exciting it was to get behind the wheel? If you were anything like me, it was something you looked forward to for months and months. In this country, driving is a privilege because there is power and freedom behind the wheel. But that is not only true about the steering wheel.

The Bible talks in different places about how God is like a potter who is making us into a masterpiece behind the pottery wheel. In case you don't know that much about pottery, it is the process of forming vessels and other objects out of clay (earth) and other ceramic materials. What happens is that a potter takes the clay or material and gets it nice and soft and moldable with water so he can shape it how he likes it. Then it is placed in a special oven where the fire will cause the soft, pliable clay to become hard and durable.

Catch all of that. God is sitting at the potter's wheel making a creation out of all of us, but the process sometimes includes going through the waters and even the fire. Sometimes when we feel like we're drowning, God is getting us moldable and soft enough to work with. We must be tried in the fire in order to be made solid and durable again. After the world tries to drown us and take us out, God's Spirit purifies and fortifies us. We don't have to be worried through the process because God is the one behind the wheel. He is the Master Potter who is not confused and doesn't make mistakes. Also, the character of our Potter is to move in a relaxed and pleasant way. He will never put more on us than we can bear.

Everything you will experience this week is part of God creating a masterpiece out of you. Best of all, good potters do their work without being hurried. In the same way, God has His own schedule and His own design plan. Just trust the One behind the wheel.

Prayer: *Lord, help me to remember that You are the One behind the wheel smoothing out every jagged edge and creating a masterpiece. Help me to submit to Your skilled hands. Remold and remake me as often as You choose. I am Yours and You are the Master Potter. In Jesus name, Amen.*

RENOVATION QUESTIONS:

1. When were you last under water or feeling the fire? How did you manage and keep your faith strong?

   _____

   _____

   _____

   _____

2. What can you tell yourself when you notice the molding and shaping process getting a little hard?

   _____

   _____

   _____

   _____

Day 6

LET THE SPIRIT LEAD

Teach me to do your will, for you are my God;
Let your good spirit lead me on level ground.
PSALMS 143: 10

Everything we do has a consequence attached to it, whether good or bad. The human experience isn't an excuse to act in a way that is detrimental to your walk with God. People like to use the phrase "I'm only human" whenever we speak and react out of our emotions or fleshly desires. When our way and our words matter more than the feelings of others – or better yet, more than how God feels, then we are not operating in the fruit of the Spirit. Jesus said, "I am the way, the truth and the life." Jesus told us this because He understands that whatever we sow is what we will reap. The way of the Spirit is opposite of our flesh and does not bend to our desires. This is why self-control is listed among the fruit of the Spirit.

It is only by the Holy Spirit that we can live peaceably with all men and achieve whatever goals we are attempting to reach. Without getting a handle on our mouths there can be no peace. If we don't discipline ourselves daily, then we can't achieve goals. Self-control is one of the biggest attributes of God, because it shows that both your mouth and your body can be controlled by the Spirit and the Spirit of God is now your only measure. We must measure everything by the Spirit in order for any goal to be reached.

If you suffer with anger, or emotional ups and downs, you should always rely on the Spirit to help you balance out those emotions. Submitting to the Spirit rather than your flesh is the only way to live a God-led lifestyle. The Holy Spirit is the only spirit that mankind will submit to without choice. It is only through the power of God's Spirit that we can live the life God has planned. It is only by the Holy Spirit that we can teach and lead others into an abundant life. Truth only comes through the Holy Spirit. If we're not teaching and helping someone through the Spirit, then we're not helping them at all. Our so-called wisdom and guidance is the equivalent of the blind leading the blind without the Holy Spirit at work.

Prayer: *Father, I thank You for the gifts of the Spirit that You have given us. Give us the wisdom to use the Spirit in every situation. Father, I pray that You give me the strength to have self-control. Father, You supply us with all that we need, and we thank You for giving us the self-control we need to achieve our goals. In Jesus' name we pray. In Jesus name, Amen.*

RENOVATION QUESTIONS:

1. What's one area in your life where you know you need to exemplify more self-control?

_____

_____

_____

_____

2. Have you ever had someone give you advice from their own wisdom and not from God? How did it impact you?

_____

_____

_____

_____

Day 7

IT'S RENOVATION DAY

Be not conformed to this world, but be ye transformed by the renewing of your mind.
-ROMANS 12:2

Today is the first time we're taking a break from our lessons for the week. I'd like for you to take moment to reflect on the past 6 lessons you've learned.

Renovation Day is all about Reflecting, Releasing, and Renewing. When you start a renovation, you must start with reflecting; observe what needs to go first. Second, you should release. Take the old and unwanted rubbish and haul it out, through prayer and repentance. Then finally, you can renew; rehearse the lesson or scripture that is essential for your new space.

Begin your Renovation.

REFLECTING:

_____

_____

_____

_____

_____

_____

_____

_____

_____

_____

_____

_____

_____

_____

_____

RELEASING:

_____

_____

_____

_____

_____

_____

_____

_____

_____

_____

_____

_____

_____

_____

RENEWING:

_____

_____

_____

_____

_____

_____

_____

_____

_____

_____

_____

_____

_____

_____

Day 8

I AM THE HOUSE

Don't you know that you yourselves are God's temple and that God's Spirit dwells in you?
1 CORINTHIANS 3:16

In the Old Testament, God dwelled in places. He always lived in things, like physical shelters. God was willing to live in the tabernacle, in the Ark of the Covenant, and in the Temple. But now in the post-New Testament era, God doesn't dwell in property, God dwells in people. God lives in us. We are blessed to be born in this time. God has chosen us to be God's house. The best part is that it doesn't just start when we understand it or when we become "worthy." God has always been inside of us; we just weren't always aware of it. That's why you hear God's voice now that you're a little older, still telling you the same things that the voice was telling you when you were younger. Remember that voice telling you not to steal that bag of potato chips or not to be disobedient to your parents? That was the voice of God, living on the inside. Now the stakes have gotten a little higher. The voice is now telling you not to sleep with that person who you know you're not married to. It's the same Spirit; God is still dwelling inside of us. In fact, God has always been speaking to us from the inside since the day we were born.

The problem is, as we grow older, we grow apart from God at the same time. As we get used to this world, we stop hearing clearly. As we spend more time here, we become susceptible to the culture, to society, and to our surroundings. Eventually God has to filter through everything you've learned and taken in over time. God's house over time becomes caked up with decay and it gets more and more unlivable...and from time to time a renovation needs to happen. That is what this season is all about. We are going to rehab this living Temple, one room at a time. Since God has chosen to live in us, the least we can do is fix up this house!

Prayer: *God, I give myself completely over to You today. You have free reign to do whatever You desire* *in me through this process. Have Your way and create what most brings You joy in me. I submit to Your design choices. I acknowledge Your full and total ownership. Be pleased to dwell in me, Lord. Your home, Your will, Your way. In Jesus name, Amen.*

RENOVATION QUESTIONS:

1. What rooms in your life have you allowed to become messy or cluttered recently? What needs the most renovation or deep cleaning (marriage, prayer life, etc.) ?

   _____

   _____

   _____

   _____

2. When was the last time you submitted to a true spiritual renovation?

   _____

   _____

   _____

   _____

Day 9

WHO LEFT THE GATE OPEN?

The lamp of the body is the eye. If therefore your eye is good, your whole body will be full of light.
MATTHEW 6:22

When he speaks to us, He speaks through our consciousness, our secret place. Most humans live subconsciously though; we react to things without knowing what is driving us and why we are doing things. We call everything instinct or human nature. We use those words to justify every impulse that comes to our subconscious. But God doesn't dwell in the subconscious. He dwells in your consciousness. He dwells in your mind, your most important asset. God speaks clearly and intelligently. God speaks directly when you are tempted. God gives extremely specific ways out of sin. God gives wisdom when we have to make hard choices. God makes His design choices plain to us; we just choose to ignore it and keep the house "as is." But we leave the gates open to other influences that get into our subconscious and start to drive us.

There are three gates of entry that we have to learn to protect if we want God to be the Center and the true Lord of our lives. You and I must guard our eye gates, our mouth gate, and our ear gates. We must keep close watch over what we say, over what kinds of music and influences we listen to, and over what we watch. These are the ways the enemy can get into the house and throw our renovation project off course. If we are careful of those three things, then our house will be prepared and ready for the Holy Spirit to dwell.

Commit today to blocking out those influences and to turning up the volume on God's internal voice. Push past what your body is saying to do, past what your friends are modeling to you, and past what the sin nature is trying to make normal. Listen and respond. God is serious about this renovation.

Prayer: *Lord God, thank You for choosing me. Thank You for allowing me to be Your Temple. I pray that You give me wisdom and understanding on what I should* *and shouldn't be watching, hearing, and saying. I pray that You increase my discernment, so that I may be aware of Your presence. Help me to close the gates and listen to Your voice only. In Jesus name, Amen.*

RENOVATION QUESTIONS:

1. What do you spend too much time listening to or watching?

2. What might your life look like if you committed to replacing one of your favorite radio stations, television shows or other influences with reading your Bible or listening to worship music?

Day 10

I CAN SEE CLEARLY

Give thy servant an understanding heart to judge thy people, that I may discern good and bad: for who is able to judge such great people?

1 KINGS 3: 9

In the field of Optometry, the term "20/20 Vision" is used to describe specific qualities of sight from a measuring system called Snellen Eye Chart. This chart illustrates the measuring system for different levels of vision. Optometrists suggest that 20/20 vision is equal to "perfect" vision. Though 20/20 vision is considered "perfect" sight in the natural world, I'd like to submit to you that there is a greater level of sight to obtain in the spiritual world. While it's a blessing to have 20/20 vision, seeing things only through your natural eyes will cause you to be spiritually blind. Natural sight isn't always the best way to assess people, places, or situations. We can't tell who's good or bad just by looking because our eyes can deceive us. We have to look through God's eyes as they're much clearer. It's as if they allow us to see things through a spiritual magnifying glass. If we see better, we have better judgement and discernment.

James 1:5 says, "if any of you lacks wisdom, you should ask God, who gives generously." How many times have we negatively judged a situation or person prematurely and ended up being wrong about our conclusion? This likely happened because we probably didn't acknowledge God in that situation. We can't recognize the full picture without wisdom and discernment. The Father wants us to get our judgement and decisions through prayer for things we don't understand, as well as the things we think we do understand. It's in Him we live, move, and have our being. Looking through God's eyes allows us to make the correct judgement every single time.

Prayer: *Father, I thank You for this great day only You can make. I'm thankful for Your grace and mercy that You so freely give me each day. I also thank You for never forsaking me when I didn't acknowledge You in all my ways. You are truly kind. Today I pray for wisdom and discernment so that I can serve and judge correctly. In Jesus name, Amen.*

RENOVATION QUESTIONS:

1. In your own words, describe the difference between seeing in the natural and seeing in the spiritual?

   _____

   _____

   _____

   _____

   _____

2. What area(s) of your life requires you to look through spiritual lenses today and how will you go about it?

   _____

   _____

   _____

   _____

   _____

Day 11

TRUTH, NOT FACTS

But when He, the Spirit of truth, comes, He will guide you into all truth. He will not speak on his own; He will speak only what He hears, and He will tell you what is yet to come.

JOHN 16:13

We all like to feel valuable and important. Psychologists figured out a long time ago that human beings have needs that are ranked from most important to least important. One of our central needs is value. That means that we all want to do something that we feel is important and valuable. This need goes back to how God made us. When God created us, God said that we are "good." We were already valuable and important. We didn't have to chase it. The book of Genesis also tells us that we are made in God's "image and likeness." We are valuable and important because God is, and we are like God.

Being filled with the Holy Spirit is a nonnegotiable for us. If you do not listen to Holy Spirit, then ministry is a no for you. The Holy Spirit is the only One who can save us from the lies of the enemy. I believe that too often we listen to and accept the world's facts and we forget that the world can only offer us facts, but God always gives us the TRUTH. Jesus promised that the Spirit of truth would guide us in the right way when we are distracted and discouraged by the facts of life. The Holy Spirit knows more than any and every psychologist, medical doctor, and theologian. He knows more than every book you've ever read or that exists on the planet. The Holy Spirit has and will bring pure truth to this earth, regardless of the temporary situations we face. Let's examine the difference between fact and truth:

Fact: My desires and wants are not all fulfilled.
Truth: God has supplied all of my needs according to His riches in glory.
Fact: Every day I wake up, it seems like life is ridiculously hard and I can't seem to get a flow.
Truth: He will keep in perfect peace those whose minds remain on Him.

Don't let the facts distract you; let the Spirit of Truth reveal what's real and eternal.

Prayer: *Lord, keep my head and heart focused on Your Truth. Remind me every day that You have the last say on what is real. Remove every distraction and competing voice that tries to speak against Your revealed Truth. In Jesus name, Amen*

RENOVATION QUESTIONS:

1. What are you watching on tv right now? Are you filling your mind with the news and with opinion pieces? What Truth did God maintain in spite of the facts?

_____

_____

_____

_____

_____

_____

_____

2. How can we fill ourselves enough with the Truth that we are not deceived by momentary facts?

_____

_____

_____

_____

_____

_____

_____

Day 12

PITY'S A FOOL

I have seen something else under the sun: The race is not to the swift or the battle to the strong, nor does food come to the wise or wealth to the brilliant or favor to the learned; but time and chance happen to them all.

ECCLESIASTES 9:11

Having compassion for someone and feeling sorry for someone are two different things. When you feel sorry for someone or for yourself, you become paralyzed. You can go into prolonged bondage and it can change your heart and your perspective. The feeling of compassion that causes us to bear one another's burdens comes from God, pity does not. I'd like to give you an example of when you are pitying someone. Hopefully, this will help you see why showing pity serves no one. You know that you are pitying someone when you just feel sorry for them, but you won't help them out of their unfortunate situation. Whether you are showing pity for yourself or others it does not help. Pity keeps you in bondage; in a place called stuck.

I remember when I used to feel low and feel sorry for myself. I remember that the more I pitied myself, the longer I stayed in the situation. When we pity or feel sorry for something or someone, we forfeit the true flow for healing or deliverance. When we pity, it's like we're saying God is not good. It is better to have compassion because compassion comes from a supernatural place. It's always whole and it's exactly what the person needs in order to get out of poverty, bondage, or whatever situation they may be in.

Compassion brings healing and freedom. When Jesus fed the 5000 or when He touched blinded eyes and they regained their sight, it came from a pure and powerful place. Pity comes from our fallen soul, but compassion is spiritual. Our emotions are temporary and fleeting, so pity is useless. But when the Holy Spirit moves us to compassion, it brings true spiritual and effective change. The point of all this is that if we want to truly worship Jesus and become the spiritual house He can dwell in, then we must have a lifestyle full of compassion just like Christ did.

Prayer: *Thank You, Father for the compassion that You have given Jesus to die on the cross for our sins. Lord, we pray for Your supernatural Spirit of compassion. We know that You are a good God and that You do not want any of us to be bound, sick, or confused. Thank You for Your compassion and Your love for us. In Jesus name, Amen*

RENOVATION QUESTIONS:

1. Has anyone ever treated you like a *pity case*?

_____

_____

_____

_____

_____

_____

_____

_____

2. How did it make you feel to be pitied?

_____

_____

_____

_____

_____

_____

_____

_____

_____

Day 13

GOOD FATHER

You Lord are our Father, we are the clay. You are the Potter, we are the workmanship of your hands.

Isaiah 64:8

For some reason mankind has been subliminally taught that God isn't pleasantly good. Goodness comes only from God the Father. When the Father made us, He made us without stress or anxiety. God created us perfectly and gave us the perfect environment for perfect enjoyment. Since we are His children we can live and grow and create without fear and anxiety too. We have to choose it though. I want us to see God as the good Father in our lives! We are His children who have been adopted into the family of Christ. When we begin to see God as a Father, then we can be much more content and at peace with our lives and with the daily decisions we have to make. Why? Because we can trust our Father's hands and heart.

There's no question that God is good, so what better Father to trust in but the good Father? The Bible tells us that we are children of a good Father over and over (For example: Psalms 100:3): *"Know that the LORD is God, it is He who made us, and we are His; we are His people, the sheep of His pasture."* This Scripture implies that God is our creator and our maker. He could have just created us and left us in a fallen state, but through Jesus Christ, He **made** us righteous.

If the good Father made us, then He knows how our minds and bodies work. Not only is God aware of who we are, but also what we need and desire. God is the one who created and set it all up. God is not surprised by what we experience nor is He unprepared to care for us. Not only does God know, but God is in this thing with us. Jesus is called "Emmanuel," meaning that God is here with us. But also, when we go back to Genesis, we see that we even share God's image and likeness. Jesus Himself says in John 14:20, *"One day you will realize that I am in my Father, and you are in me, and I am in you."* We even share God's spiritual DNA! The Good Father has given us everything we need because He is good.

Prayer: *God, thank you for giving me everything I need to have victory on the inside and on the outside. Help me to live each day knowing that You are with me inside of my secret place. In Jesus name, Amen*

RENOVATION QUESTIONS:

1. What is something you don't have that you spend too much time thinking about? What can you spend time being grateful for instead?

_____

_____

_____

_____

2. Name one thing that God did for you that nobody else could've done.

_____

_____

_____

_____

Day 14

IT'S RENOVATION DAY

Be not conformed to this world, but be transformed by the renewing of your mind.
ROMANS 12:2

Today we're taking a break from our lessons for the week. I'd like for you to take moment to reflect on the past 6 lessons you've learned. Renovation Day is all about Reflecting, Releasing, and Renewing. When you start a renovation, you must start with reflecting; observe what needs to go first. Second, you should release. Take the old and unwanted rubbish and haul it out, through prayer and repentance. Then finally, you can renew; rehearse the lesson or scripture that is essential for your new space.

Begin your Renovation.

REFLECTING:

_____

_____

_____

_____

_____

_____

_____

_____

_____

_____

_____

_____

_____

_____

RELEASING:

_____

_____

_____

_____

_____

_____

_____

_____

_____

_____

_____

_____

_____

RENEWING:

_____

_____

_____

_____

_____

_____

_____

_____

_____

_____

_____

_____

_____

_____

Day 15

TAKE RESPONSIBILITY, NOT CREDIT

For I know that in me (that is, in my flesh) nothing good dwells, for I have the desire to do something right but how to perform what is good I do not find.

ROMANS 7:18

In the beginning of time, God created the heavens and the earth as well as the first man and woman: Adam and Eve. With everything God made, He said it was good. But when He created man, He declared it to be *very good*. Adam and Eve were the first of their kind made perfect in the image of God. It wasn't long before those perfect human beings would disobey God. Prior to their sin against God, they were good. God had made them perfect just like Him. Yet when they sinned, their hearts became filled with carnality. If you read Romans

8:6, you'll see that it tells us that the carnal mind is death (separation from God). As a result of this, there's now no good thing that lives in our flesh besides the Holy Spirit, which leads me to my next point.

Whenever a child of God does "good", we are not doing it in our own strength. Instead, we are doing it by the power of God through Christ that is dwelling within us. Since we know it isn't us performing it, we must not take credit for anything good. Because good is relative, we will have to take the responsibility to make sure we're following the Spirit. The word says, "The Spirit will lead you and guide you into all truth" (John 16:3). We must take responsibility in giving credit to the performer, Jesus. He makes the difference in producing "good' through us.

Even Jesus knew not to give Himself credit for what the Father was doing through Him. When Jesus was performing miracles and teaching in the synagogue, people would call Him "good teacher". In turn, He would ask "Why do you call me good?" Jesus knew to give God the Father all the credit for all the good He had done during His time on Earth. Jesus was quick to tell people that it wasn't Him performing the good but it was His

Father in heaven. Do you see how even Jesus gave credit to His Father? We must humble ourselves and follow Jesus' response to being called "good". Humility and honor to God is our responsibility. Be responsible for good but don't take credit for it.

> **Prayer:** *Father, I thank You for creating me. I thank You for Your Spirit which leads and guides me. I pray that You continue to help me perform all that You require of me through the power of Your Spirit, and that when I do, that I would always remember that everything good in me is from You. Thank You for always hearing me when I pray in Jesus' name. Amen.*

RENOVATION QUESTIONS:

1. Have you tried to perform or do good without the help of the Holy Spirit and failed? Please explain.

_____

_____

_____

_____

2. Where in your life can you take more responsibility in allowing Christ to perform those good things for a definite win?

_____

_____

_____

_____

_____

Day 16

THE LITTLE THINGS

Indeed, the very hairs of your head are all numbered. Don't be afraid; you are worth more than many sparrows.

LUKE 12:7

God is our true Father. We all have biological fathers, however none of our fathers know little things like the number of hairs on our head. We've all heard the old saying, "God don't make junk." Well, even if it's not good grammar, it's definitely good theology. Our Father only makes good things, and He only creates masterpieces. For God to know the number of hairs we have on our heads tells me that He is well acquainted with His creations. Since God took the time to make you, you must be important, and you meet a need in the Earth. God knows exactly why He made you. No matter how you got to this Earth, you could not have gotten here without God's permission. You are not a mistake; you have always served a purpose in the Earth.

Mankind should be extremely grateful that God the Father desires a close relationship with us. There was a time when I desired a relationship with my biological father, but he didn't share the same desire for me which was not a good feeling. But God Himself does want a personal relationship with all of us. It is fitting to respond to God because He cares about even the little things concerning you. You are the most important creation that ever existed. We should talk with the Father everyday about the things we don't know because He knows all things. The Father is willing and waiting to grow a close relationship with you right now. It doesn't matter what your nationality, gender, age, or lifestyle is, God loves you. God wants to relate to us. If we come to the Father, He said He will in no way reject us. God desires to care for us, shape us and make us into His image. We are too special and valuable to go through the journey of life and not be connected to the one who made us. We have free access to go to the manufacturer and ask for specific instructions on who we are and why we're here. God has invested too much into us for us to live beneath our Kingdom privileges and below our calling. I wouldn't go another day without communicating with God.

> **Prayer:** *Father God, teach us to humble ourselves. We know that we can ask you anything and everything. You told us to ask and it shall be given, seek and we shall find, knock and the door will be opened to us. We thank you that we can come boldly before your throne of grace, and that there is no middleman between us. I pray that you enlarge our capacity to be more aware of your presence in us, and we also thank you for being a good Father. In Jesus' name we pray. Amen.*

RENOVATION QUESTIONS:

1. What is something special about you that you sometimes overlook or forget about?

   _____

   _____

   _____

   _____

   _____

   _____

2. Take a moment and imagine what your family would be like if you didn't exist. Write a note to yourself about how essential you are to the people who love you.

_____

_____

_____

_____

_____

_____

Day 17

WHO GOD WANTS

For I know the plans I have for you,' says the Lord.
They are plans for good and not for disaster, to
give you a future and a hope.
                                        JEREMIAH 29:11

God is not confused about who we are and who He
wants us to be. God is absolutely clear. It's us who
get it twisted sometimes. God has known from the
very beginning that He has the perfect plan for us.
And what do you do when you need information
and someone else has it? You ask THEM! The first
step to know what God wants me to be is to get to
know God and ask Him. The better connected we
are to God, the clearer our destiny becomes. When
we attempt to relate to God through our leaders,
parents or even our friends' relationship with Him,
we miss the plan and purpose He has set for our
journey. You should desire to know what God has

perfectly designed for you and only you. You can be a pastor, a bishop, a boss, a mother, or father, or even the president and not be who God wants you to be. It would be wise to consult the source of our gifts and our very lives if we desire to operate correctly.

Have you ever tried to make something for the first time and didn't follow the recipe closely enough? Or tried to put together that kid's bike and not paid attention to the instructions? It usually becomes a disaster. We need to consult the manual which shows the manufacturer's perfect design. I'm sure you already know what I mean! We can't become what God desires without a relationship with God and God's Word. It takes both.

We need the Word of God and the God of the words. If we come to church or read the Bible and never press into connection with God, then we are only reading and learning about history. This is how we turn into religious pretenders which leads to having the form of godliness but denying the power. The power is in relationship.

Remember what we learned from the garden. We are supposed to be growing and maturing like plants, and that requires constant work. We have to be sowing seeds into our spirits and pruning away temptation and tending the growth all the time. It's not a "when we have no other choice" kind of life. In my recent studies, I have learned that the reason why we don't see much fruit in our lives is that we read the Bible usually when we are unhappy, mad, hurt, sad, or depressed. This is where our problem comes from. We must learn to read the Bible when we are free spiritually and mentally. When you read the Bible through inspiration and you are free, then it's easier for the spirit to flow through you to get in your heart and in your mind. That's when God can get a Word in and change us from what we are to what we are supposed to become.

Prayer: *Lord, replace my plans with Your plans. You know me and have perfectly prepared a path for me. Help me to find and enjoy the path that runs directly through Your heart. Help me to walk so close to You that I will not make wrong turns on this journey of purpose. In Jesus' name. Amen.*

RENOVATION QUESTIONS:

1. What did you want to be as a little kid? Did God give you that dream, or did you create it yourself?

   _____

   _____

   _____

2. How can you help young people around you know that God is in control and that they can trust His plans?

   _____

   _____

   _____

3. Pray and ask God what the plan is for this week. Listen quietly for the answer and write down what you hear.

   _____

   _____

   _____

Day 18

GROW UP

When I was a child I spoke as a child, I thought as a child, I understood as a child but when I became a man/woman I put away childish things.

1 CORINTHIANS 13 :11

Growing and developing physically happens according to the laws of nature – seemingly without any effort on our part. Growing and developing mentally, however, is a direct result of desire to mature and evolve. Consequently, we don't naturally grow out of immature thinking; we have to work at it. Change isn't always easy. Letting go of immature thoughts, feelings, and behaviors requires time, focus, and endurance. During my 40-day journey with God, I learned that it actually wasn't other people holding me back from my purpose or who I needed to be, but it was me. I learned that no one had the power to keep me from becoming the woman I desired to be except for me.

In Corinthians, Paul talks about putting away childlike thinking and moving towards a more mature state of mind. This prevents us from feeling stagnant and unproductive, and allows us to take advantage of new mercies every morning so we can start new every day.

As we actively pursue this mindset, we realize that our future is between us and God, and that our relationship with our Father will equip us with the tools we need to continue to move forward. Whenever we are confused and frustrated about life and the progression of it, we can talk to the Father in the secret place of our hearts. He will give us the insight and wisdom on what to do and how to do it, and ensure that we do not stop ourselves from being who He created us to be.

Prayer: *Dear Jesus, I thank You for being my own personal Lord and Savior. I thank You for being an example for me at Your young age of 12 years old. I pray that You would help me to be aware of my spiritual immaturity and give me the wisdom and strength to know when to put away childish and old thoughts that would keep me from growing and moving forward in life. I pray that You will give me the mind of Christ and* *provide me with all the tools and content I need to mature the way You intended me too. In Jesus' name. Amen.*

RENOVATION QUESTIONS:

1. After reading this lesson, in what area(s) of your life do you realize you lack growth and maturity?

_____

_____

_____

_____

2. What are some of the ways that you can use your faith to become the man/woman you desire to be?

_____

_____

_____

_____

THE NEW SELF

That you put off your old self, which belongs to your former manner of life and is corrupt through deceitful desires, and to be renewed in the spirit of your minds, and to put on the new self, created after the likeness of God in true righteousness and holiness

EPHESIANS 4:22-24

When we talk about the "old self," where do we start? And how do we meet the new self? Self is the substratum or the basis of all relationships. When we were born, we were born with a natural affection for sin. Sin was the reason we couldn't dwell with God because sin was equal to death, or separation from God. Our sinful nature is what kept us from walking in the true image and likeness of God the Father. As a result, there was no way we could relate to the holiness of God, which is why we must put off our old selves and put on our new selves.

Our first responsibility is to take off the old self, and put on the new self like you put on your physical clothes. The Bible says that, "if any man be in Christ he is a new creature (Self) old things are passed away, behold all things are new"(1 Corinthians 5:17). For a season, it was difficult for me to realize I had been dressed in my old fashions. I had not yet taken off my old clothes which represented my old way of thinking. I needed to transform my mind by reminding *myself* that I was a new creature in Christ, and that He gave me power to do so. I had to focus on not only taking off the old self, but also renewing my mind with new thoughts for the new self. Renovating takes action, and only you can do it for *yourself.* Yes, it's ok to have people there to reinforce what you're already working on, but YOU will have to be the manager of your own process and progress. Be consistent, and practice these steps until you see your new SELF walking in the image and likeness of God. It may feel difficult at first, but remember what the Bible says in Philippians 4:13: "I can do all things through Christ who strengthens me."

Prayer: *Father, I thank you for this new day, I thank*

you for giving me tools and strategies to defeat the enemy of my mind. You have always given us a way of escape. I thank you for desiring a relationship with me. I'm happy I can talk to you at any time of the day and you will be right there to respond. I pray for strength to take off my old me and put on the new me, in Jesus name I pray in Jesus name, Amen.

RENOVATION QUESTIONS:

1. Are you able to envision the next version of yourself? What does your new self look like?

_____

_____

_____

_____

2. What if you came to the realization that the new you is waiting on you? What should you trade in order to step into your new self?

_____

_____

_____

_____

Day 20

AS THY SELF

Jesus said unto him, Thou shalt love the lord your God with all your heart, soul and mind. This is the first and great commandment. And the second is like unto it, Thou shalt love thy neighbor as they self.

MATTHEW 22:37-39

In my world, we were taught that if you love and take care of others, God will love you and take care of you. It was almost taboo to love yourself because you were seen as selfish and self-serving. I have since learned that God always intended for us to love ourselves as well as others. We are to love and respect all of His creations, including ourselves. The Bible says to love your neighbor *AS* you love yourself. So then the question is not *if* we should love ourselves, but *how* do we love ourselves?

Love is simply a choice that cannot be expressed without God. God had to show me that it wasn't a sin to love myself. He tells us to love our neighbor as ourselves because He knows that most people will love themselves, and also love others as a result. This sort of love doesn't require us to be emotional, either. In contrast, this love that God teaches us about is sobering, wise, and planned. We are loving ourselves perfectly when we get up every morning and follow our daily self-care regimen. We are loving ourselves when we are treating ourselves well, eating healthy foods, purposely being inspired, and seeing ourselves better day by day.

We cannot fear loving ourselves. John 4:18 says, *"perfect love casteth out all fear, there is no fear in love."* When we love ourselves, we are loving the masterpiece that God fearfully and wonderfully made. If we fear loving ourselves, then we begin to hate ourselves, and our self-hate will become the Devil's playground. Don't be afraid to ask God to show you how to love purely, for there is no fear in love.

Prayer: *Father, I thank You for making me perfect. I ask You to help me to love myself, as well as others, the way you intended in the beginning of time. I thank You for fearfully and wonderfully making us all. I pray that You give me the fruit of the Spirit so that I can perfectly love myself and others without fear. In Jesus' name I pray. Amen.*

RENOVATION QUESTIONS:

1. Do you find that it is easier or more difficult for you to love others? Explain why?

_____

_____

_____

_____

_____

2. Have you ever struggled with the guilt about loving yourself?

_____

_____

_____

_____

_____

3. What reinforcements will you implement in your daily routine to show more self-love.

_____

_____

_____

_____

_____

_____

Day 21

IT'S RENOVATION DAY

Be not conformed to this world, but be transformed by the renewing of your mind.
ROMANS 12:2

Today we're taking a break from our lessons for the week. I'd like for you to take moment to reflect on the past 6 lessons you've learned. Renovation Day is all about Reflecting, Releasing, and Renewing. When you start a renovation, you must start with reflecting; observe what needs to go first. Second, you should release. Take the old and unwanted rubbish and haul it out, through prayer and repentance. Then finally, you can renew; rehearse the lesson or scripture that is essential for your new space.

Begin your Renovation.

REFLECTING:

_____

_____

_____

_____

_____

_____

_____

_____

_____

_____

_____

_____

_____

_____

_____

RELEASING:

_____

_____

_____

_____

_____

_____

_____

_____

_____

_____

_____

_____

_____

_____

RENEWING:

_____

_____

_____

_____

_____

_____

_____

_____

_____

_____

_____

_____

_____

_____

_____

Day 22

TRUE COMPASSION

"For we have not a high priest that cannot be touched with the feeling of our infirmities; but one who has been tempted like as we are..."
HEBREWS 4:15

God is love. We experience God most clearly when we experience His compassion. Compassion is so important because it's how God shows His love toward us. When people show compassion, they are reflecting God. Compassion is important because it's what keeps the Kingdom system working. Compassion is a strong concern for the sufferings or misfortune of others. It's kingdom and it doesn't come to us naturally. It comes from God.

As humans, we are naturally selfish. We naturally think about ourselves first. We run away from harm, not to it. We look out for number one and then we check on others after we are out of harm's way. Compassion makes us operate a little differently though. It is an active response to something or someone. Compassion is intentional, active, and unselfish. In some ways it's like faith, you must do something to activate it. Everything about Jesus was seasoned with compassion. The choice to leave Heaven and come here is all about compassion. Jesus did most of His miracles out of compassion. Martha cried to Jesus because she felt sorry because her brother had died. But when Jesus raised Lazarus from the dead, He didn't do it out of pity. He did it from a place of compassion and purpose. Jesus doesn't heal out of pity or emotion; He responds out of compassion. Jesus waited three days to heal Lazarus. I believe He waited because he wanted to show us that we are to respond to the needs of others from a place of true compassion.

Believers should be full of compassion but not pity. We have to be careful when we start to pity and feel sorry for people or for ourselves. God has given us all a measure of faith, along with supplying all of our needs according to His riches. You are not someone's source, God is.

Prayer: *Father, whenever I am tempted to operate in pity instead of compassion, remind me that You love us*

*and have provided for all of us through Your Son. Help
me to be like Jesus, to be selfless and intentional in
seeing and supporting somebody else. In Jesus' name.
Amen.*

RENOVATION QUESTIONS:

1. What are some ways you have experienced Kingdom compassion recently?

   _____

   _____

   _____

   _____

   _____

2. Name a time when you had pity on someone, and God helped you to establish better boundaries?

   _____

   _____

   _____

   _____

Day 23

CHECK YOUR FLOW

"Above all else, guard your heart, for everything you do flows from it."

PROVERBS 4:23

Maintaining boundaries is one of the most important lessons to learn in this life. Boundaries are used to protect your heart from things that can hurt you and to put a demarcation between your property and someone else's. We are responsible for our own self-care. I didn't realize that I neglected to protect my own heart, which caused my heart to be contaminated. Luke 6:45 says that, "out of the abundance of the heart the mouth speaks," meaning whatever you allow to affect you will come out of your mouth. Growing up, I was one of those people who had a problem ready for every solution. About 99% of my thoughts were negative against myself. That negative thinking poisoned every part of my life. The well in my heart was full of bitter water so everything in my life turned bitter too. It all starts with the heart. It's like if you have a water tank in your house full of contaminated water: every shower, every time you brush your teeth, every time you cook with that water—you are being contaminated. You can't help it, what's in the water source is going to flow out. That's why it is important to be mindful of what you think on daily.

It was when I began to renew my mind with the word of God, when I got to the point of speaking Word and speaking life, that my life started to change. I had to learn to use my faith. I had to learn to check what was flowing inside of me and replace the source.

It's time to start guarding your heart. Stop letting people dictate your worth. Put the Word in the flow! Stop letting bad situations convince you that God has forgotten you. Put the Word in the flow! True happiness begins when we replace the anxious, negative voices with hearing the Word. Let's use worrying as an example. Personally, I don't think men worry as much as women. Women are always expected to have it all together, so we worry when we don't think we can meet the expectations placed on us. We let the voice asking for perfection get to us. We need to put a gate up between that voice and our hearts. Shut that voice down that says to worry. Turn up the voice of God saying, "Can all your worries add a single moment to your life?"

True happiness is to live in the moment; to regulate your heart. Regulating things means putting limits on access to them. Everything can't flow into your heart because it's going to eventually flow into your home and your family. Shut it down before it messes with your flow.

Prayer: *Lord, help to regulate what goes into my heart and flows into my life. As I walk through this day, help me to take inventory of every thought and take it captive by Your blood. Let the life You desire for me take shape in me today, beginning in my heart of hearts. In Jesus' name. Amen.*

RENOVATION QUESTIONS:

1. Do you have a decorative picket fence, a midsized privacy fence or a fully armored 20-foot wall around your heart?

   _____

   _____

   _____

   _____

2. How has leaving your heart unguarded left you open to attack and heartache?

_____

_____

_____

_____

Day 24

WHERE ARE YOUR RIVERS?

The Lord God planted a garden eastward in Eden, there He put the man whom He had formed. And out of the ground the Lord God made every tree grow that is pleasant to the sight and good for food. The tree of life was also in the midst of the garden, and the tree of the knowledge of good and evil. Now a river went out of Eden to water the garden, and from there it parted and became four riverheads.

GENESIS 2:8-9

About 20 years ago I took up a skill called landscaping and I'm amazed at how much it has taught me. I've learned so much about life, about God, and about how humans are directly connected to the earth and the materials in it. We can learn so much from studying how God created the world. From the very beginning, God was intentional and generous with us. God created the garden and placed us in it. God provided Adam with all that he needed but left it up to man to dress and keep it. From the beginning God has expected us to be gardeners, and to put time and effort into growing things He created. Part of being human is putting in the work for personal growth and to grow and care for the things God has given us. Growth and maturity don't always come easy, but God commanded it. He knows our abilities and doesn't ask us to do what's impossible. Do you remember when Jesus is seen by Mary Magdalene after the Resurrection? She saw Jesus and assumed He was the gardener. Jesus was teaching us to care for things that others would overlook. In the same way, we all look most like Jesus when we are intentionally cultivating the things God gave us dominion over.

God was so committed to man being successful in this work that God provided everything we needed. God even intentionally placed rivers in the garden to be sure Adam had everything he needed. God does the same thing with us. Everything we need God places in our midst, and God never gives us "just enough." God didn't put one or two rivers in the garden; God provided four rivers! In other words, He gave them MORE than enough.

Let that be a reminder to you today: God calls us to work and take care of what we have, but

God doesn't leave us alone and empty-handed to do it. Look over the garden of your life today and count your blessings and resources. I believe you will recognize at least four gardens God has given you. Locate your rivers and get to growing.

Prayer: *God, help me to recognize the calling to occupy, subdue, and care for the Earth around me. You have given me everything I need through your Son's blood and through your constant presence within me. Help me to reflect Your own nature as a Creator and Sustainer. Teach me to see the rivers and to do the work. In Jesus' name. Amen.*

RENOVATION QUESTIONS:

1. What are some of the rivers God has placed in your life (people, gifts, etc.) to help you fulfill your purpose?

_____

_____

_____

_____

_____

2. What do you need to "dress" and "keep" this week? Are you neglecting any of your territory? If so, how are you going to work on it?

_____

_____

_____

_____

_____

Day 25

YOU GROW GARDEN!

"And God blessed them. And God said to them,
"Be fruitful and multiply and fill the earth and
subdue it…"

GENESIS 1:28

It wasn't a coincidence that God placed man into a garden in the beginning. In nature it is easier to understand the purpose and plan of God. God always desired for man to grow, to mature, to blossom and to create something beautiful out of life. In Genesis 1 and 2, we see words like increase and fruitfulness, and also images of things "bursting forth." God doesn't desire for us to be stagnant. He wants us to produce, just like plants do. That's why He placed us in a garden as a metaphor to see what we should become.

Many of us want to please God in our lives, but we must be mindful that a major key for pleasing

God is to be fruitful and multiply. Being fruitful and multiplying isn't just about making babies however, it's more about being productive within your everyday life. God wants us to grow spiritually, intellectually, and emotionally. God wants us to branch out and become more than what we were yesterday. Growth is part of the human design. If you want to see the Creator smile, then you must be fruitful. God wants us to be fruitful and our territory to multiply. That's why we are promised that He will withhold no good thing from those who walk upright.

God wants us to be happy, but what many don't know is that happiness comes from trust, knowledge and understanding. We can only truly be happy as we grow in how we trust God and God's plan and timing. John 1:2 says, "Beloved I pray that you would prosper (or grow) and be in good health even as your soul prospers (or grows)." We become truly happy as we get to know God the creator better. We begin through a relationship with God to understand that He is for us and is working all things out for good to them that love Him. Mankind often gravitates to performance level service to God because we like to feel useful. Sometimes we spin our wheels trying to **do** as much as we can, but God isn't just concerned with what we do. He's concerned with who we're growing into. God has planted you in His garden called life, so take root and bear fruit. Be fruitful and multiply. It's time to grow!

> **Prayer:** *Lord, don't let me miss any chances to grow and transform today. Growth is always difficult, but I desire to become all You want me to be. Let me transform into a disciple who truly trusts and rests in You. In Jesus' name. Amen.*

RENOVATION QUESTIONS:

1. What are some growing edges in your life? What places do you need to let God expand you in?

_____

_____

_____

_____

_____

_____

2. What are the biggest barriers that get in the way of your trust in God? Do you recognize how they keep you from being truly happy?

_____

_____

_____

_____

_____

_____

3. Can your life this year be described by words like "fruitful," "increase" and "bursting forth?" If not, what do you need to do differently?

_____

_____

_____

_____

_____

_____

Day 26

LEMONADE

"I think myself happy..."

ACTS 26:2

Happiness is a state of mind that all humans strive to obtain. I don't know anyone who doesn't love to be happy. But whenever we're not happy we may instinctively want to blame others. How many times in life have we blamed our state of mind on another person or situation? I was one who thought whatever negative state I was in at that time was related to what I had been through, or felt it was someone else's fault. Many people are suffering with depression, hopelessness, anger, and other emotional dysfunctions. For some reason in this culture, we're not taught to take the responsibility to protect our own hearts (our emotions). The culture also teaches us that happiness comes from accomplishments, or the way we are treated by others. I learned that my happiness and my state of mind was my responsibility, and if I was to blame someone for my state of mind, it should be me. I remember thinking my unhappiness was other people's fault, until I read the story about Ruth and Naomi.

Naomi was Ruth's mother-in-law. Naomi had recently experienced a series of unfortunate events. Her husband and her two sons had passed back to back. Naomi grew bitter because she was unhappy about what had happened with her family. Naomi became so bitter that she changed her name to Mara (which means bitter). She believed that bitterness would be her portion for the rest of her life. Hebrews 12:21 says to "lay aside every weight and sin that so easily besets us." This means let us rid ourselves of everything that blocks the prosperity of our souls. Bitterness is a weight which can also lead to sin. It leads to sin because it can cause us to miss what God intended for us. Weights and sins block us from seeing the beam in our eyes and cause us not to view others correctly.

With Christ we can live a happy, unbothered life. Christ is the perfect *sweetener* to add to your heart. It is possible to live to the point where nothing negative affects us. For we know that all things work together for good. The lemons of life are bitter, but when you sprinkle a little sweetness on it, it will bring out a beautiful flavor.

Prayer: *Father, we thank You for Your grace and Your mercies that You give us each day. Father, we pray and we thank You for forgiveness of our sins and weights that beset us. Lord, we pray that You strengthen us to not allow bitterness or unforgiveness to control our lives. We thank You that we have Your peace, and that we have the power to forgive just as You forgave us. In Jesus' name. Amen.*

RENOVATION QUESTION:

1. Do you have a habit of blaming your negative experiences on other people?

_____

_____

_____

_____

_____

_____

2. How can you allow God to make you better
   and not bitter in this season?

   _____

   _____

   _____

   _____

   _____

   _____

Day 27

CHEER UP!

"These things I have spoken unto you, that in Me ye may have peace. In the world you will have trouble; but be of good cheer, I have overcome the world."

JOHN 16:33

For most of my life I have operated in stealth mode. As a child, I was quiet and shy, very afraid to do anything in front of anyone, and hated to speak in any type of public setting. Because of this, I learned how to survive on the bare essentials of life, and never needed or asked for much of anything – ever. It was so bad that people often asked my mother if I was mute, or if I communicated with anyone else besides her. I can imagine how uncomfortable answering those questions must have been for my mother. But honestly, if I met a child now who talked as little as I did then, I would probably be asking the same questions.

As an adult, God has revealed to me that not speaking was a result of crippling anxiety and unhappiness, rooted in the absence of my biological father in my home. Because of this, I lived my whole life subconsciously fearing and doubting everything and everyone. I often felt vulnerable and unprotected, and lacked the confidence and security that comes with the consistent presence of a parent or guardian in your life.

In the Scriptures, Jesus tells us that we have no reason to be anxious or worried because He is with us always. When the Bible tells us to cheer up, it is simply saying put away our doubts, fears, and confusions because Jesus has all Authority! He has all power! Taking joy and being cheerful every day is the way that the Father wants His children to live on this earth. He wants to know that we believe in Him and that we trust Him when He says the battle is already won!

Prayer: *Father, I thank You for overcoming the world before I was even born, and I'm grateful that I can walk this earth without fear. From this moment forward I will neither walk in fear nor doubt anything You have promised me. I will always remember that You, my Father, made me and love me eternally. In Jesus' name. Amen.*

RENOVATE QUESTIONS:

1. Has the absence of an important person such as, your mother, father, husband/wife contributed to your lack of joy and peace?

_____

_____

_____

_____

_____

2. Is there anywhere else in your life where you find yourself subconsciously fearing and doubting the unknown? If applicable, explain your scenario. How can you trust God more?

_____

_____

_____

_____

_____

Day 28

IT'S RENOVATION DAY

Be not conformed to this world, but be transformed by the renewing of your mind.

ROMANS 12:2

Today we're taking a break from our lessons for the week. I'd like for you to take moment to reflect on the past 6 lessons you've learned. Renovation Day is all about Reflecting, Releasing, and Renewing. When you start a renovation, you must start with reflecting; observe what needs to go first. Second, you should release. Take the old and unwanted rubbish and haul it out, through prayer and repentance. Then finally, you can renew; rehearse the lesson or scripture that is essential for your new space.

Begin your Renovation.

REFLECTING:

_____

_____

_____

_____

_____

_____

_____

_____

_____

_____

_____

_____

_____

_____

RELEASING:

_____

_____

_____

_____

_____

_____

_____

_____

_____

_____

_____

_____

_____

_____

RENEWING:

Day 29

FEARLESS

Do not be anxious for anything, but in everything by prayer and supplication, (humbly asking) with thanksgiving making your request known to God, and the peace of God will guard your heart and your mind in Christ Jesus.

PHILIPPIANS 4:6-7

Anxiety is defined as intense worry about everyday situations and decisions. There are many reasons anxiety rears its ugly head. They can include conflict, heath issues, death, false beliefs, and spiritual attacks. No matter the cause, anxiety puts us in a fearful state of mind, the kind that interrupts our day to day activities. For me, anxiety and fear were the foundation of my thoughts. It was the way I processed life. Even as a child, it was the main emotion that left me unproductive for years. I was afraid to do just about anything. Not only did fear paralyze me, it also caused sickness and disease. Like many others who suffer from it, it also wore on my body and mind. I was the first partaker and I became sick from an anxiety disorder that I developed over time.

God doesn't want us to fear anything because He made all things. Colossians 1:16 reads, "For in him all things were created: things in heaven and on earth, visible and invisible, whether thrones or powers or rulers or authorities; all things have been created through him and for him," therefore we have nothing to fear. The command "Fear not" is mentioned 365 times in the Bible. Once for each day of the year. Fear is a major challenge in every believer's life. The enemy knows this, and forms weapons that instigate fear in our lives. The devil understands that if he can put fear in your heart, then he doesn't have to fight you on a daily basis. The fear will take root and do his work for him. Isaiah 26:3 promises that God will keep those who trust Him, those whose minds are stayed on Him in perfect peace. But we must remain focused. Without a doubt, the Father wants us to keep our mind on Christ because HE is our example and the reason we have access to peace. Don't you want to take advantage of that peace? After all, how much easier is it to keep your mind on one person, Jesus, rather than trying to keep up with the millions of thoughts and issues that run through your head. Get into the habit of keeping your mind on Jesus and the peace of God will protect your heart and mind in all things.

Prayer: *Father, I thank You for this great day You've made. You have given me new mercies every day of my life. You are a gracious God and Your perfect love is the reason I'm alive today. I pray that You will help me get rid of all my fears and anxiety. I'll do what Your word tells me to do. I'll keep my mind fixed on You because You can and will protect me. From today forward, I believe that You are with me wherever I go. I give You thanks in Jesus' name. Amen.*

RENOVATION QUESTIONS:

1. Do you struggle with anxiety in certain areas of your life? If so, identify what those areas are.

_____

_____

_____

_____

2. Has fear kept you from being productive in any way? What strategy will you use against fear from now on?

_____

_____

_____

_____

_____

Day 30

PERFECT PEACE

You keep him in prefect peace whose mind is stayed on you, because they trust in you.

ISAIAH 26:3

When we talk about peace, we must begin with the mind. The mind is the most important asset we have to assist us in producing the quality of life we all hope for. How can we live a quality life without peace? We can't. We can only have things like peace when we set our mind to it. Peace doesn't just show up; it has to happen on purpose.

Proverbs 23:7 says, "As a man thinks in his heart so is he." That means we have the power to think positive or negative about anything. Think of the mind like fertile ground: we will reap what we sow. If we plant fruit, we will produce fruit. If we plant poison, we will produce poison. The same is true for peace and fear. Fear and doubt are the enemy's most common ways to get us off the course of peace which keeps us anxious for everything. If we think on fear constantly then we will produce it.

My personal belief is that the only way to have peace is to passionately trust God. In reading Jeremiah 29:11 we can see that He has our best interest at heart. Perfect peace comes from rehearsing the truth over and over and over. Christ is the Prince of Peace. Keeping Christ on our mind HAS to produce the peace, the kind that passes all understanding. Before Christ died, He said "my peace I leave with you." Jesus knew that the goal of the enemy was to steal the peace that Christ so graciously left to us. We can't go a lifetime trying to be Christ-like without possessing His perfect peace. It is a necessity for life. In this lesson today, I hope you begin to see that your peace of mind is the most important asset you will ever invest in. Remember to keep your mind on things above where Christ sits on the right hand of the Father. Let the peace of God dwell in you richly. He has the perfect peace.

Prayer: *Father, I thank You for being the All-Knowing God. I also thank You for leaving me with the comfort of peace. You are a good God; You always know what* *to do for Your children. I pray that You will continue to keep me in perfect peace as I keep my mind fixed on You in Jesus' name. Amen.*

RENOVATION QUESTIONS:

1. What thing(s) have you allowed to disturb the peace in your life and why?

   _____

   _____

   _____

   _____

2. What should you do to better preserve and protect your peace? You may refer to the lesson in developing your response.

   _____

   _____

   _____

   _____

Day 31

THE PERFECT GENTLEMAN

Behold I stand at the door and knock. If anyone hears my voice and opens the door, I will come in to him and eat with him, and he with me.

REVELATION 3:20

Ladies, we all know there is nothing better than being with a man who is an absolute gentleman. When you find the man who was "raised right" and doesn't mind pulling out chairs, picking up the tab, and holding doors open consistently, you have found something great. His kindness and gentleness tug on our hearts because they are reflections of the first example of a perfect gentleman we know: God. The traditional picture of a perfect gentleman is a man putting his jacket over a puddle for you to walk over, protecting you from the stains and residue of mud. God didn't just place His jacket in the mud for us; He placed His Son on the cross for us, protecting us from the stains and residue of sin! *The Perfect Gentleman.*

But some of us, because of broken pasts with broken people, don't appreciate the Perfect Gentleman. We are so accustomed to negative behaviors (being controlled, disrespected, or treated unfairly) that we learn to accept those behaviors as the norm. But that's not the character and nature of God. God is good! He has all power and control, yet He knocks and gives us the choice to let Him into our hearts. He is kind and gentle when dealing with our hearts. We need to let go of our distorted views of acceptable behaviors, and look to God as an example of how others should treat us. We must embrace unconditional love by letting God, the Perfect Gentleman, into our hearts.

Prayer: *Lord, heal my heart from any religious guilt and habit of trying to earn Your love. Minister to my soul through Your Word this week so that I come to know Your kindness and gentleness. Remind me that You shed Your blood out of love and You want me to shed my fear and guilt. In Jesus' name. Amen.*

RENOVATION QUESTIONS:

1. What bad things have you brought into your relationship with God from other relationships (with your parents, siblings, partner, or spouse, etc.)?

   _____

   _____

   _____

   _____

   _____

2. Is your relationship with God tainted by guilt or traditionalism? How can you let that go?

   _____

   _____

   _____

   _____

   _____

Day 32

LAW-ABIDING KINGDOM CITIZEN

Do not think that I have come to abolish the Law or the Prophets; I have not come to abolish them but to fulfill them.

MATTHEW 5:17

For thousands of years, God our Creator has been trying to find a way to redeem us back to Himself. When Adam and Eve disobeyed God in the garden, that released a curse/death that pushed us as far from communicating with God as possible. For a long time, God has been coming up with different strategies to redeem us, but none of the strategies worked until he sent his son Jesus to pay for our sins and redeem us back. When Jesus came, he was the perfect payment for all of our sins.

Without Jesus, we were not able to keep the laws of God. Do you remember the Ten

Commandments? Well when I researched a little bit deeper, I found out that there were actually hundreds of commandments for the children of Israel. God gave them chance after chance to keep those commandments but His creation was not able to keep the laws on their own. But the Good News is that when Jesus was born and came on the scene, He fulfilled the law. He became the Law-Abiding Citizen for us. Now the Spirit of Jesus, the Holy Spirit, lives inside of us. God said He has written His law on our hearts and our minds, to make it easier for us to abide by them. Christ is the fulfillment of the Law. He is the Word made into flesh. We're not desperately trying to keep the Law on our own; Christ is inside of us doing the work in us.

We also now have grace, so if we do break the law or the rules, Jesus Christ is there to put things back together again on our behalf. We can thank Jesus for all of the sacrifices that He made for us to be free to communicate and commune with the Father again.

Prayer: *We thank You Jesus for all of the sacrifices that You made for us, to fulfill the Law that we could not keep. We are grateful for Your compassion on us. Help us to rest in Your blood sacrifice, rather than living* *our lives in self-righteousness. Thank You for helping us realize we cannot keep the Law on our own, but we need Your grace and mercy to become the Law-Abiding Citizens You've called us to be. In Jesus' name. Amen.*

RENOVATION QUESTIONS:

1. Read Leviticus chapters 17-19 this week and see some of the laws God gave to the people of Israel.

   _____

   _____

   _____

   _____

2. Have you ever tried to change yourself in your own strength without relying on God's help and leaning into God's grace? What was the result?

   _____

   _____

   _____

   _____

3. Write yourself a letter this week about your journey to Christ and at the end list three things you need to give over to God to change in you that you have not been able to change on your own.

_____

_____

_____

_____

Day 33

BETTER

See what great love the Father has lavished on us, that we should be called children of God! And that is what we are.

1 JOHN 3:1

When I was dealing with the pain of not having my biological father around as a girl, I was embarrassed for a long time. If I'm honest, for years of my life I was constantly embarrassed, sad, and pitiful about it. But when God spoke to me in my adult years, He told me something I have never forgotten. In a dark moment when I was wondering why, I remember God telling me that this way was better because of the purpose He had planned for me. Imagine that: God said it was better for me! It took a long time to receive and understand that truth, but now I believe this for every stepchild, orphan, or misused person. When others leave, abandon, or hurt you, who better to guide and love and care for you than your heavenly Father? God has always been with all of His children since the day we were born. He is the only one who has never left us. Some of us have had the privilege of having Him as our primary influence and place of peace. When others drop the ball, we are forced to rely on Him, and He is the perfect Father.

Once I got that revelation, I was grateful, joyful, and happy to realize that God had been taking care of me the whole time. I had the privilege and the honor of not having an earthly father in my life, because God was my Heavenly Father and had a plan for me all along. My Father was always available, never broke His promises and provided perfectly for my every need.

At the end of the day He's your true Father. If you didn't grow up with a father in your home or if you grew up with a father who was abusive or not a good father, God was always there. Receive it. Never feel shameful, guilty, or pitiful about your past. You have a heavenly Father that will never leave you nor forsake you.

Prayer: *Father, I thank You because You knew what was best for me before I came to this Earth. I thank*

You for having a plan for me even when I was in my mother's womb. Like Jeremiah, You know the thoughts and plans You have for us, plans of good and not evil. Thank You. In Jesus' name. Amen.

RENOVATION QUESTIONS:

1. Have you ever tried to make something happen on your own but realized in the end that God had something better planned?

   _____

   _____

   _____

   _____

2. How has God blown your mind and exceeded your expectations?

   _____

   _____

   _____

   _____

Day 34

THE KING'S TABLE

Blessed are those who hunger and thirst for righteousness, for they will be filled.

MATTHEW 5:6

As a little girl, hunger was something I didn't feel often. I was so thin that people used to ask my mother if I had some type of eating disorder. During that time, I felt fine. As time went on, I began to lose energy. I became weak and tired and slept all the time. I hardly had any drive or zeal. My lack of hunger affected my quality of life. As a result, it was extremely difficult to focus in school, at church, or any place I attended for that matter. I realized then that both food and drink are necessities for a healthy and thriving life.

God created us to eat and drink both spiritually and naturally. God blesses those who hunger and thirst not only after natural food but spiritual food too. He knows that if we only hunger and thirst after natural things that we won't be fully satisfied. Full satisfaction comes from natural food and spiritual food, so that both the body and soul are fed. Do you remember when Jesus said "I thirst "when He was hanging on the cross? He was physically thirsty, but also yearning for the Spirit of God which He felt leaving His body. Jesus needed both and so do we.

God is so good to us that He has given us full access to all that He is. Jesus told us in the Scriptures that His body was broken for us to eat of it, and commanded us to eat of His flesh and drink His blood. He equates His body to bread and His blood as wine in order to show us that if we eat and drink of Him, then we will never be hungry or thirsty again. However, if we only eat and drink what the world has to offer, we forfeit full satisfaction of true peace and fulfillment. Only Jesus can give us all we need to live a full, happy, and healthy life. Jesus is sitting at the table waiting for us to commune with Him and to share His grace and love to all who believes. Eat from the bread of life.

Prayer: *Lord Jesus, I thank You for all of the sacrifices You have made for me. I also praise You for dying and* *being the ultimate sacrifice for me to be able to share in Your sufferings and also being able to commune with You. You are the true and living God and I am more than grateful to be able to eat from Your table of grace. Father, from this day forward I will receive Your body as my bread and Your blood as my drink. In Jesus' name. Amen.*

RENOVATION QUESTIONS:

1. How often do you feed your spirit? Can you take the challenge to feed your spirit just as often has you feed your natural body?

_____

_____

_____

_____

2. What method(s) will you now use to get your spiritual nutrients?

_____

_____

_____

_____

Day 35

IT'S RENOVATION DAY

Be not conformed to this world, but be transformed by the renewing of your mind.
ROMANS 12:2

Today we're taking a break from our lessons for the week. I'd like for you to take moment to reflect on the past 6 lessons you've learned. Renovation Day is all about Reflecting, Releasing, and Renewing. When you start a renovation, you must start with reflecting; observe what needs to go first. Second, you should release. Take the old and unwanted rubbish and haul it out, through prayer and repentance. Then finally, you can renew; rehearse the lesson or scripture that is essential for your new space.

Begin your Renovation.

REFLECTING:

_____

_____

_____

_____

_____

_____

_____

_____

_____

_____

_____

_____

_____

_____

RELEASING:

_____

_____

_____

_____

_____

_____

_____

_____

_____

_____

_____

_____

_____

_____

RENEWING:

_____

_____

_____

_____

_____

_____

_____

_____

_____

_____

_____

_____

_____

Day 36

BIG FAITH

Without faith it is impossible to please God, because anyone who comes to him must believe that he exist and he rewards those who diligently seek him.

HEBREWS 11:16

When God asks us to do something that's too hard or seemingly impossible, He's never asking us to do it alone. I had to learn over the course of the journey to use my faith when asked to do anything concerning Godly things. God's not asking us to do anything in our own strength, but He wants us to believe that He will give us the strength to do it. When God called me to undergo consecration for 40 days, I didn't know what to expect. God told me after the 40 days of wilderness, that He would speak to me on another level then He did previously. I thought it would be 40 days of praying, reading, and researching before I heard one thing from God. To my surprise, it didn't take Him 40 days to get me to the place where he wanted me. On day 3 of the journey, I heard God's voice like I had never heard it before. He started speaking immediately.

Most people don't move forward into better things because they fear they won't be able to commit or they don't have faith that the Father has something better for them. God told Abraham to kill his only son! Abraham loved his son, but Abraham was willing to lean on his faith and trust that God knew best. He was willing to sacrifice his son, and would have if God hadn't stopped him and provided a ram in the bush as a substitute sacrifice. This is all the more proof of the power of having big faith! If we are willing to do what God has asked us to do, He will meet us where we are, and continue to protect and provide. The Father wants to know if we will obey and trust Him no matter what. God deals with us the same, He always has a ram in the bush for us if we're willing to trust Him. When I took this 40-day transformation journey, I had to believe that God would give me the strength and the power to commit, and before I knew it I was hearing His voice more clearly and seeing myself through His eyes. I also had the strength to complete the 40-day journey. When God asks us to do something that's challenging for us, He's asking us to do it to build our faith in His word and to build our trust in Him. The Father will always give you the tools, strength, and strategy to do whatever it is He's asking you to do. Your decision to obey and trust God is the only way that you can access the new you.

> **Prayer:** *Father, I thank You for another day. Another day to get to know You better. Teach me Your ways and give me the strength I need to grow my faith, help me to realize that I can't please You without faith. From today forward I will move at your command without fear of the unknown. Thank You for all of Your benefits You've graciously given me, in Jesus' name. Amen.*

RENOVATION QUESTIONS:

1. What does having BIG FAITH look like to you?

_____

_____

_____

_____

_____

2. What is the BIGGEST FEAR you've had, and how did you conquer it?

_____

_____

_____

_____

_____

Day 37

SOUL MANAGER

Like a city whose walls are broken through is a person who lacks self-control.

PROVERBS 25:28

Self-control is one of the most important gifts from God. It will be absolutely necessary if we want to achieve the goals we have set for our lives. Self-control gives us the ability to manage our actions, feelings, and emotions. We are most like Jesus when we show self-restraint and can control our emotions. At the Garden of Gethsemane, Jesus was our perfect example. When Jesus was later arrested by the Roman soldiers, unlike His disciple Peter, Jesus showed amazing self-control. Peter had the opposite reaction. He became so angry that Jesus was being arrested, that he cut off the ear of a Roman soldier. But Jesus had compassion on the soldier and immediately healed him. Then Jesus warned Peter that if he lived by the sword he would die by the sword.

Every day, we make decisions as to whether we will control our impulses and responses or whether we won't. As we renovate our Temples, Jesus wants us to manage our lives as He did.

God's Spirit is at work in us. It creates fruit that validates us. In order to be like Him, we must be Spirit-led and Spirit filled. Self-control is the evidence of God at work, renovating this Temple from the inside out.

Prayer: *Please help me to always show self-control by remembering to stop, think, and pray before I act. I don't want to be like a city without walls that allows everything in. Help me to regulate how I respond and to keep my eyes on You. In Jesus' name. Amen.*

RENOVATION QUESTIONS:

1. Would people describe you as a self-controlled person? Would you describe yourself that way?

_____

_____

_____

_____

2. Journal today about what self-control would look like in various parts of your life.

_____

_____

_____

_____

Day 38

PURE GOLD

*These trials will show that your faith is genuine.
It is being tested as fire tests and purifies gold—
though your faith is far more precious than mere
gold. So when your faith remains strong through
many trials, it will bring you much praise and
glory and honor on the day when Jesus Christ is
revealed to the whole world.*

PETER 1:7

The value of a person isn't based on the things they possess, neither is it based upon the people they know. Our American culture subliminally teaches us to care for things that make us "look good" instead of putting emphasis on being good from the inside out. We often set our focus on things that are not worth our time because those things don't test us. We like to take the easy road, but being tested and tried by the Holy Spirit is what make us strong in our faith, and allows us to be good from the inside out. We are like gold, a natural metal that has been processed through fire to seal and protect the integrity of the metal. The trying of gold in fire is what brings the most value to it, and the same is true for us as well.

That trials that come to test our faith are life situations provided by God. Although these trials can be hard to endure, they don't come to kill us. As a result of the trials, we learn more about love, patience, peace, and joy; eternal gifts of the Spirit that are more precious than gold. These trials also prove us and strengthen our faith walk, bringing us closer to God.

Colossians 3:2 tells us to set our affections on things above. As we overcome these trials, we begin to focus less on finding value according to the world's standards and begin to realize that our value is in something that comes from a far greater source. It is important to understand that our true value can only be measured by the Holy Spirit and that we can only depend on God to increase our value! God loves His creation. He knows what's best for us.

Prayer: *Father I thank You for Your goodness to me. I'm honored to serve such a brilliant being. You've planned* *my life from the beginning of time. All of my gifts and talents come from You because You are my source. I've learned today that my value is in You. Please forgive me for esteeming things over You. Help me to understand that it is You who provides life situations to test my faith and make me stronger. Thank You in Jesus' name. Amen.*

RENOVATION QUESTIONS:

1. What area(s) of your life are on fire (where do you find yourself being tested)?

_____

_____

_____

_____

2. Can you identify spiritual things that can grow stronger in this fire?

_____

_____

_____

_____

3. What spiritual fruit can you concentrate on developing while being tried in this fire?

_____

_____

_____

_____

Day 39

LIVING TRUTH

Let the words of my mouth and the meditations of my heart be acceptable in thy sight, O Lord my strength and my Redeemer.

PSALM 19:14

One of the most frustrating things for parents is when kids lie to you. For one, nobody wants their kids to be liars and dishonest. But on a different level, it is frustrating because you can always tell when they are lying. Parents know the truth and we usually know our kids' behaviors that give it away every time. We know our kids. It's the same thing between us and God. God loves honesty because He knows everything anyway. God knows the things we don't know and even those things we don't feel comfortable saying out loud.

Culture teaches us to say "yes" when we want to say "no." Over time we learn how to say what people want to hear or what won't hurt anyone. It's not just the larger culture, but the church culture as well. When we were growing up, there were times in our lives when the wrong people attempted to speak into our lives and they would tell us that if we didn't do what they said, whenever they said it, that we were wrong and in sin. I now know this was a form of manipulation.

No one should ever force you to do something that you don't want to do! God doesn't even force us. Like a good gentleman, God knocks on our heart and waits for us to accept or reject. Nobody should manipulate and force us into things. And neither should you do that to yourself! You have to guard your heart and be honest about what you're feeling at all times. When I am open and honest with myself and when I let myself feel how I feel, it is easier to tell others. We must let our yes be yes and our no be no, but it takes work. Our hearts and our words must match in order for them to benefit us and bless God. Doing things out of obligation is not God's way. When we make vows to God, God wants us to keep them out of gratitude and passion. Fear-based religion will destroy your joy and hope. Grace-filled submission will change your life.

Prayer: *Father, I pray this day that You help me to speak the truth in love, and I also pray that I will not fear anyone to the point where my heart and my mouth don't match. Give me the strength to tell the truth and to always be honest with myself and others. In Jesus' name I pray. Amen.*

RENOVATION QUESTIONS:

1. What things do you say to convince yourself that it is okay to ignore what you really want and think?

   _____

   _____

   _____

   _____

2. Why do we sometimes tell "little white lies?"

   _____

   _____

   _____

   _____

KEEPING YOUR VOWS

When you make a vow to God, do not delay in fulfilling it. He has no pleasure in fools; fulfill your vow. It is better not to vow than to make a vow and not fulfill it. Do not let your mouth lead you into sin.

ECCLESIASTES 5:4-6A

My wedding day was one of the most beautiful days of my life. Standing before God and making those vows was a holy and beautiful moment. However, the real work begins when the last dance is done and all the decorations have been taken down. Keeping vows is a job that lasts forever. The Bible teaches that it's better to not make a vow than to make one and break it. In other words, it's better not to make a vow at all if we are not really committed to keeping it, because making vows and not meaning it is false pretense. Also, when you make a vow and don't keep it, you throw off the integrity of the commitment altogether.

When you do make a vow, that means you make a sacred agreement with someone or something. If you make vows and choose not to hold up your end of your bargain, you cheat the person who made the vow with you which is not fair to them. That's why honesty from the beginning is the most important part of any relationship or connection.

As much as we hate to admit it, lying and breaking our word comes naturally to us because of our sinful nature. No matter how we try to excuse it, lying is a sin and when we say we're going to do something and don't do it we lie to ourselves and the person. We must mean what we say. Our words and our hearts must match. That's what God loves. The word says, "Out of the abundance of the heart the mouth speaks." So, let's fill our hearts with truth so that we can speak truth and not violate our word and bond.

Prayer: *Father, please give us the strength to remain faithful to the vows we have made. When life's challenges cause us to give up on what we have said, help us to remember that You are with and in us, giving us strength to keep our word. In Jesus' name. Amen.*

RENOVATION QUESTIONS:

1. Has anyone ever broken a major promise to you? How did the betrayal make you feel?

   _____

   _____

   _____

   _____

   _____

2. What promises have you broken to God that you need to go back and fulfill?

   _____

   _____

   _____

   _____

   _____

FINAL NOTE TO THE READERS

To all my Renovators:

I truly hope you were able to find some time to take the 40-day Journey Renovation Challenge. If you completed the whole journey, you have officially become a 40 Day renovation expert in transforming your mind. Being transformed isn't always easy but, you pushed through and stayed focused. You should feel great about your accomplishment!

If you've been able to see change and progression in your faith, then you should take all you've learned and share it with your friends, and family.

This book is your own personal progress report reminder. You can always refer back to the book when you feel yourself slipping back into an old way of thinking. If needed, you can take the full challenge all over again. If there's no need for you to start from the top, then you can go to any chapter in the table of contents.

Remember that Jesus Christ is the only way to a true relationship with the Father. You are a RENEWED creature in Christ.

My Prayer: *Thank you Father for your grace that helps us to be able to finish what we have started. I thank you for every single person who read this book and experienced growth in their life. I believe that all of what was written in this book was inspired and accepted by You. I pray that my 40-day journey was an eye-opener to your kingdom citizens. I pray a supernatural blessing for all who read it in Jesus' name. Amen.*

www.ingramcontent.com/pod-product-compliance
Lightning Source LLC
Chambersburg PA
CBHW060752100426
42813CB00004B/790